Sew a Row Pro

Karin Hellaby

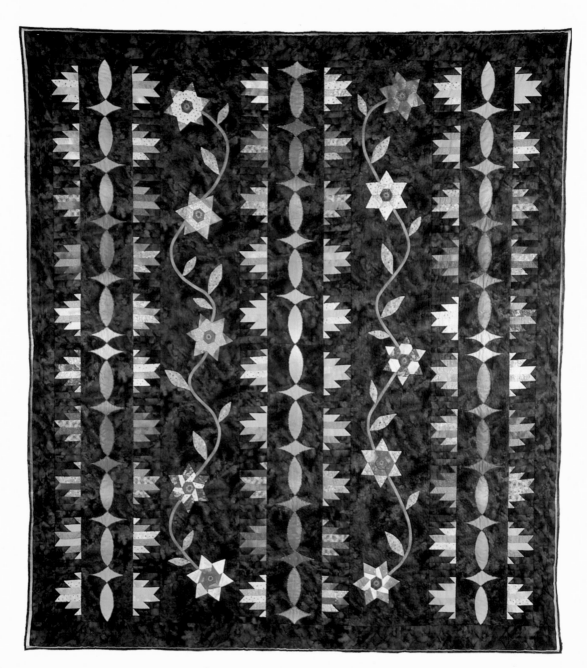

A companion book to Sew a Row Quilts

Quilters Haven

Publications

Acknowledgements

This book is dedicated to all my students throughout the world – old friends and new! Without your help, comments and sewing skills this book would not exist.

Once again Rosemary and Allan have exceeded my expectations with their ideas on diagrams and layout. It was a new experience for me to be an assistant to a photographer and Neil worked fast in difficult circumstances.

Finally thanks to Steve Smith, my liaison with our new printers. He made my project managing so much easier by answering any queries with 'no problem, we can do that'!

First published by
Quilters Haven Publications in 2003

Copyright © Karin Hellaby 2003

Graphics by Rosemary Muntus
Layout by Allan Scott

Photography by Neil Porter, Oaklands
32 Old Sneed Park, Stoke Bishop,
Bristol BS9 1RF

Printed by Borcombe SP
Premier Way, Abbey Park Industrial
Estate, Romsey, Hampshire SO51 9AQ

ISBN 0-9540928-2-1   UPC 7-44674-60520-7

Quilters Haven Publications
68 High Street, Wickham Market
Suffolk IP13 0QU, UK

Tel: +44 (0)1728 746275
Fax: +44 (0)1728 746314

www.quilters-haven.co.uk

Sew a Row Projects
Karin Hellaby

Page 1: Enchanted Valleys
by Karin Hellaby.

Page 3: Baltic Brights
by Karin Hellaby.

Left: Christmas Quilt
by Julia Reed.

*Bottom: Funky folder and quilter's
tote bag by Pat Matthes.*

4

Contents

Introduction

Two years ago my first book, Sew a Row Quilts, was published. I was thrilled when it was so well received throughout the world.

I was invited to teach at the prestigious Houston Quilt Festival. For these classes I designed some unique patterns as multi-technique Sew a Row projects. There was tremendous interest in the patterns, and they have become the inspiration for this book. Why a book? Because, as I said at the time, 'Why produce three individual patterns when we can have five times as many in a full colour book for no difference in price?' Obviously I was wearing my shop owner 'hat'!

Please note: it is essential that you have a copy of Sew a Row Quilts alongside this book when you are working on any of these projects!

The symbol SaR followed by a page number refers to the instructions in the first book.

Please read everything carefully. If anything is new to you, cut and sew one block first. And do remember that despite all the testing, checking and proof-reading that we do, mistakes can occur in any book.

If you wish, you may photocopy and enlarge any of the black and white quilt plans in the book, and colour them in to help you finalise your own choice of fabrics.

Wherever possible, colour variations of the same design have been made to inspire you. I hope you will enjoy sewing projects from this book, and that it will become a stepping stone for you to create your own designs.

Suffolk is blessed with quaint English seaside towns which look as if they belong to a bygone era. Little seems to have changed in the past 50 years. This 28" x 33" quilt is based on the beach huts at Southwold, a town that is popular with holidaymakers. All the beach huts are privately owned and very rarely come on the market. When they do they fetch phenomenal prices.

Seven Ways to Sew a Row was the title of the first class I taught at the Houston Quilt International Quilt festival, and this quilt was made as the class project. Students from the Netherlands, Israel and other countries told me that beach huts like these are familiar to them. Wherever you live, why not personalise this project to remind you of glorious childhood days at the seaside?

7

Fabric needed

Sky – ¾ yard

Sea – ½ yard

Border and binding – ½ yard

Yellow – ¼ yard

Orange – ¼ yard

Roof (3) Huts (3) Kites (3) –
9 different fabrics, use scraps
or ⅛ yards

QH tip

Use crow footing (S&R
page 94) to depict birds
in the sky.

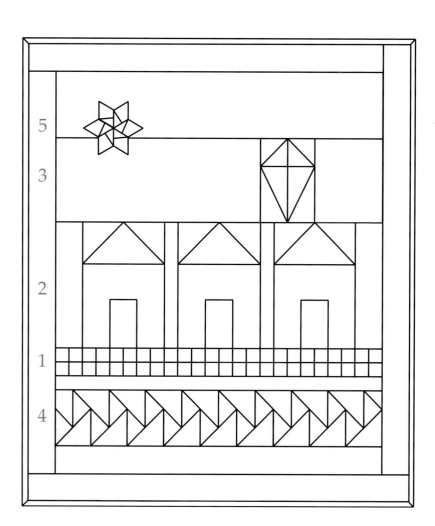

Instructions

Rows are arranged horizontally.

1 Chequerboard Beach

(See S&R page 20). Cut two 1½" strips, one in
yellow and one in orange.
Stitch along length.
Cut into 24 x 1½" squares.
Stitch into chequerboard row.
Press.
**This row will dictate the width of all
patchwork rows.**

2 Beach Huts

Cut three 6½" squares in three fabrics.
Doors: cut 3 doors, each 4" x 2¼".
Appliqué into position.

3D Geese – S&R page 39. Beach hut roof: for
each roof cut one goose (6½" x 3½") and two
3½" background squares.
Stitch to top of beach huts.
Use two 1½" x 8½" strips of sky fabric to
separate beach huts. Join huts into row.

Cut two strips of sky fabric (each 2½" x 8½")
and stitch to each end of huts row. Sew to
beach row. Trim ends even.

3 Kite

Half Square Triangles – S&R page 31.
Cut two 2⅞" squares of sky and one 2⅞"
square in each kite fabric.
Sew into two half square triangles.
Stitch together.

Skinny Triangles – S&R page 35.
Cut two sky pieces (4½" x 2½") and one 4½" x
2½" piece in each kite fabric.
Sew into two mirror image blocks.
Stitch together. Sew units into kite.
Complete row by adding 6½" wide sky strip to
either side of kite. Sew to huts row.
Trim row ends even.
Stitch a 5" wide sky strip above kite row.
Trim row ends even.

4 Sea and Fish

Migrating Geese – ЅaR page 42.
Use 4″ finished width.
Fish – cut five 3⅞″ squares.
Sea – cut one 3⅝″ strip, cut into 11 squares.
Sew 18 fish into a row.
Add extra sea if needed to match rows.
Cut 1½″ sea strip. Sew to bottom of beach.
Add the fish row.
Cut 2½″ sea strip. Add to bottom of fish row.

5 Sun

English Patchwork – ЅaR page 65.
Cut a half strip in yellow (2¾″). Cut a half
strip in orange (1½″).
Stitch together along length.
Use medium diamond template (1½″) and
cut six. Stitch as on ЅaR pages 66-67.
Appliqué to sky.

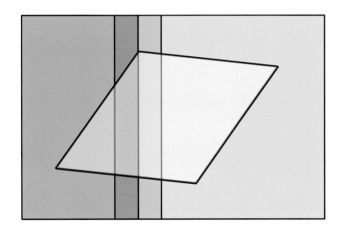

Exact size template for sun, shown in position on sewn strips.

6 Finishing

Border – ЅaR page 84. Cut four 2½″ strips.

Layer and quilt. The sea is quilted with
wavy lines. Beach huts are quilted in the
ditch around each square. Crow footing
(ЅaR page 94) is used to depict birds in the
sky. Meander quilting is used in the sky. A
ribbon and bows are stitched to the kite.

Binding – ЅaR page 98. Cut three 2¼″ strips.

Sky and mountains stitched as in the quilt
plan below. Use half square triangles where
sky and mountains meet. Appliqué trees,
bears, moose and salmon using the templates
on the next page. Trace designs onto the rough
side of a sheet of freezer paper. In the case of
the trees, trace one side, fold along the centre-
line, flip over and trace the other side.

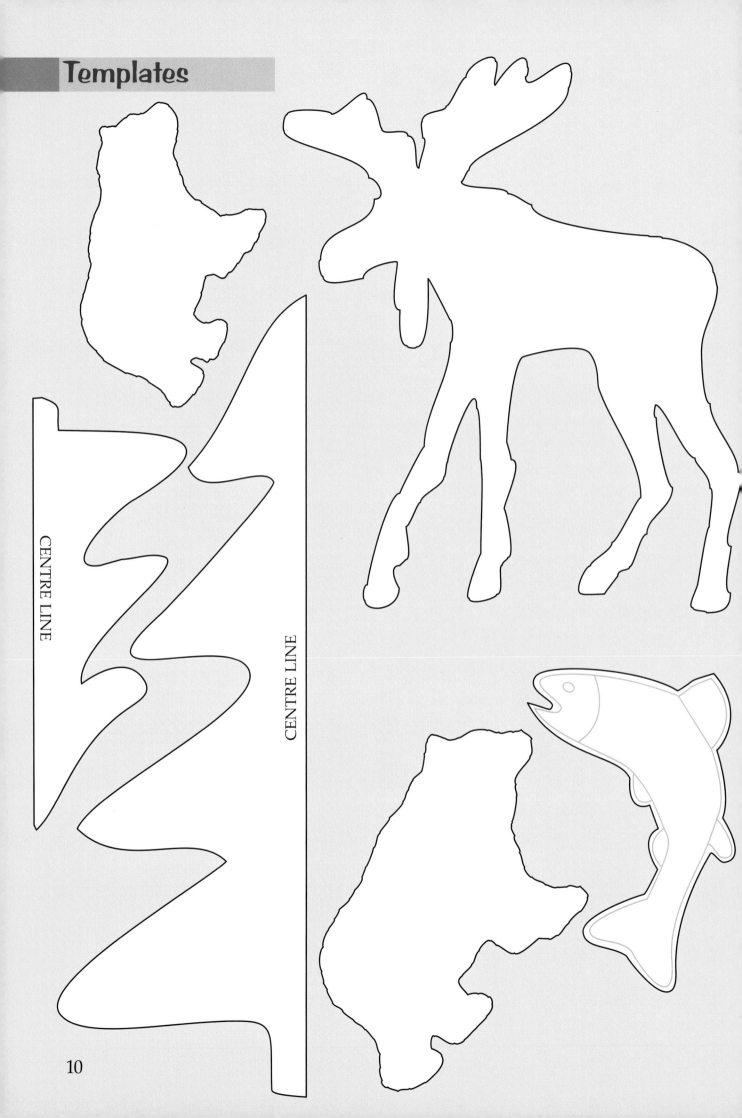

CENTRE LINE

CENTRE LINE

Quilters often find their gardens an inspiration for their quilts – clematis growing up against stone walls, sunflowers blowing in the breeze. During summer months when the weather is fine many quilters find a conflict between the beckoning garden and their stitching needs.

So why not combine the two by using long summer evenings to make your garden-inspired quilts?

Sheila Marr's 28" x 32" quilt was inspired by a blue clematis close to her kitchen door. Now she can see her clematis in bloom throughout the year.

11

Fabric

Flowers – ⅛ yard (or scraps) for each, in purples or blues

Greens – various, ½ yard total

Stone wall background – ¾ yard

First border – ¼ yard

Second border and binding – ½ yard

Instructions

Rows are arranged vertically.

Cut six 4½" squares in various greens.

Cut two 8½" background strips, width of fabric. Cut into one 26½" length, one 22½" length, one 18½" length.

1 **3D Geese – SaR page 39**

Make six geese using six green rectangles and 12 background squares.

2 **Easy Stems – SaR page 62**

Make three 14"–17" lengths to use as flower stems.

3 **Leaves – SaR page 64**

Cut out 12 leaves using leaf template.

4 **Dresden Daisy – SaR page 70**

Make three Dresden Daisies.

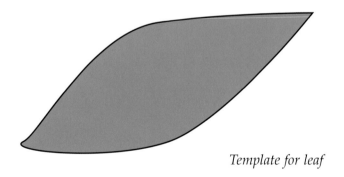

Template for leaf

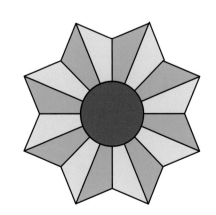

5 Assembly

Row 1: Stitch two geese together and stitch to base of 26½"-long background strip.

Row 2: Stitch two geese together. Stitch two green squares together. Stitch geese to top of squares, and stitch this unit to base of 22½"-long background strip.

Row 3: Stitch two geese together. Stitch four green squares together. Stitch geese to top of squares and stitch this unit to base of 18½"-long background strip.

Following quilt plan, appliqué stems and leaves in place on each of the three background strips.
Appliqué one Dresden Daisy to the top of each stem.

Stitch rows together as in quilt plan.

6 Finishing

First border – cut 1¼" strips and stitch to quilt top.

Second border – cut 2" strips and add to quilt top.

Layer, quilt and bind.

Top: Sunflowers *by Pam Bailey.*

Bottom: Baltic Brights *by Karin Hellaby uses multi-coloured fusible bias binding for the stems and leaves.*

Button it Down!

I wanted to make a contemporary quilt using black and white alongside some of my favourite solid colours. I chose a weekend when I could stay at home as a supportive Mum to my 18-year-old son, who was studying for his final exams.

He decided to spend most of the time out socialising! Rather than rant and rave I felt it was diplomatic to 'button it'. When I found the buttons, the quilt had to be called 'Button it Down'. I am glad my own exams were a long time ago!

14

Fabric

White – ¾ yard

Black – 1 yard, includes borders

Colours – ½ yard of each of four colours
(blue, turquoise, purple, pink)

Buttons – 36

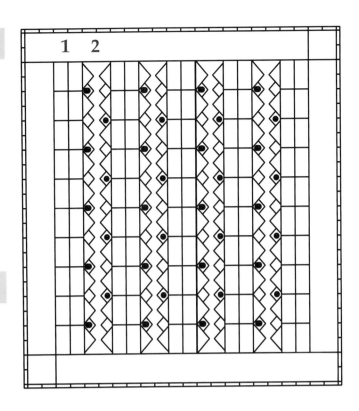

Instructions

Rows are arranged vertically.

1 Chequerboard – SaR page 20

Cut six 2½" strips from white
Cut six 2½" strips from black
Stitch along length. Press. Cut into 4½" units.
Stitch ten units into chequerboard length to
make one row. Repeat to make five rows.

2 Prairie Points – SaR page 96

Cut two 4¼" strips from each of four colours
to make four prairie point lengths.
Follow **What if...?** on SaR page 97. Take two
contrasting strips and sew along length.
Press seam open.

Continue by turning strip into a length of
prairie points that look like 'tulips', following
instructions from step 2 (SaR page 96). The
second folded square becomes the 'bud' by
not enclosing the triangle base inside the
fold.

The prairie point length is complete when
there are 10 large triangle folds, with nine
buds between.

Cut four 4½" x 40½" black strips. Stitch a
length of prairie points to each side of black
strip, placing raw edges together with points
facing to centre of strip.

Use buttons to stitch down alternating buds.

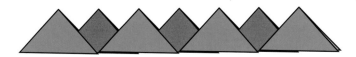

3 Assembly

Stitch vertical rows together, alternating a
chequerboard row with prairie point row.
Finish with a chequerboard row.

4 Border

Cut two 40½" x 4½" black strips.
Stitch to quilt sides.
Cut two 44½" x 4½" strips.
Stitch a 4½" white square at one end of
each black strip.
Attach to top and bottom of quilt.

5 Layer and quilt

The quilt is 'stitch in the ditch' along each
vertical row.

The border is quilted using the triangle design
of the prairie point as a stencil.

6 Binding

Stitch a strip set using alternating colours, in
2½" strips, press seams open. Cut into 2¼"
binding strips and use to bind the quilt. Two
sides of the quilt have been bound in blue/
turquoise and two sides in purple/pink.

15

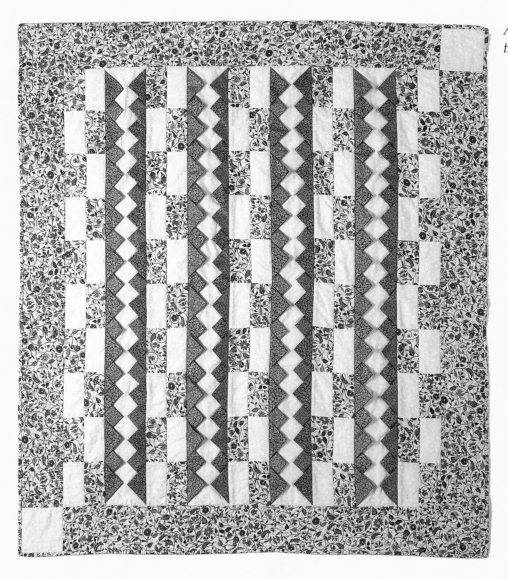

A variation on the original theme by Heather Langdon.

Close-up of the original **Button it Down** *quilt.*

What if...

...you make your rows horizontal rather than vertical?

...you insert prairie points only on one side of the plain rows?

...you use ribbons or tassels instead of buttons?

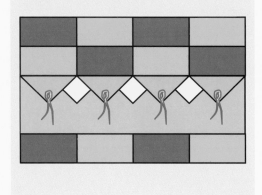

16

Sew-a-Row Blues

A quilt that reminds us of Delft china. Pat Matthes took only a few weeks to make this quilt, and found it great fun to design: the magic Sew-a-Row formula ensures that all the rows line up, even though several different techniques are used. When we saw this quilt we knew it had to go in the book: we loved the asymmetrical effect of her design! The combination of blocks is particularly clever, making it look as if an L-shaped border has been added. If you're not comfortable with this, it's easy to add some more 'border' blocks around the centre rows of the quilt to create symmetry. Traditionally, quilts in this style were made to be used on a bed placed next to a wall. Pat has included a row of log cabin squares, a variation on the courthouse steps featured in the original *Sew-a-Row Quilts*.

Fabric

Half and quarter yards
in various blues, creams
and whites.

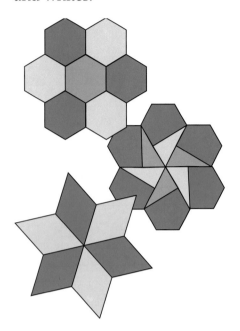

Instructions

Rows are arranged horizontally.

8" blocks are used throughout.
Eight blocks make one row.
There are ten rows.

1 **Courthouse Steps or Log Cabin –
SaR page 26**

Make six blocks.

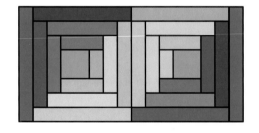

2 **Greek Keys – SaR page 28**

Make six blocks.

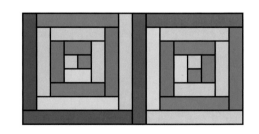

3 **Down the Patchwork Path –
SaR page 44**

Make 18 blocks; each block has four 4" units.
The units are made from a background light
square with a dark circle.
Make 12 blocks.
The six end blocks have the four units in a
different arrangement.
Stitch six blocks to make a row. Make three
rows.

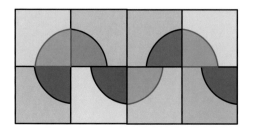

18

4 In the English Tradition – S&R page 65

Make 12 blocks – four hexagons (1″ size), four diamonds (2″ size), two split hexagons (1″ size) and two split diamonds (2″ size).

Appliqué each to a light background square.

Stitch six blocks to make one row. Repeat.

5 Chop Suey – S&R page 22

Make 24 blocks (only 23 are needed) Use four 12½″ strip sets.
Six blocks are used to make one row.
Eight blocks are used to make bottom row.
Remaining blocks are added to the end of the first nine rows, following quilt plan.

6 Appliqué – S&R page 56

Cut 15 x 4½″ light background squares for centre appliqué.
Appliqué nine hearts, four stars, two outline hearts, one on each square.
Cut 180 x 2½″ squares from light and dark fabrics.
Stitch 12 squares around each appliqué square.

QH tip

Cut 9″ background squares – and when you have finished the appliqué, trim squares to the correct 8½″ cut size.

Seven blocks are used to make this row. Remaining blocks are used in the first eight rows.

Finishing

Stitch rows together following quilt plan. Layer, quilt and bind.

Heart template for the appliqué design in Sew-a-Row Blues.

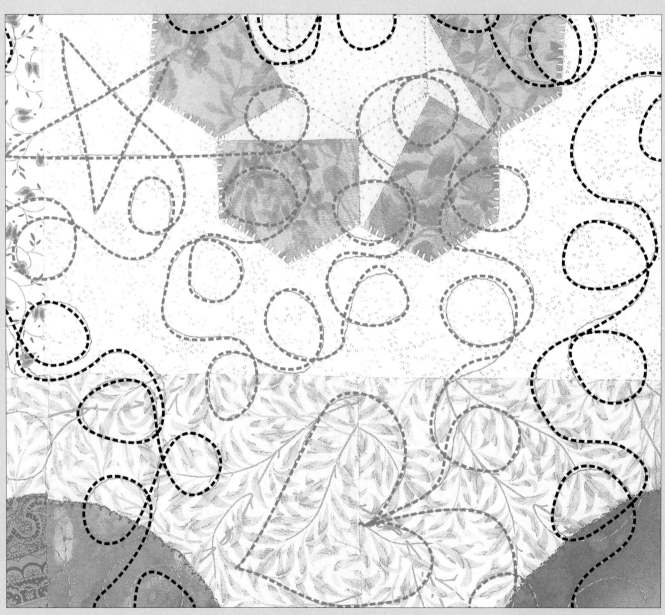

Detail of the machine quilting used for Sew-a-Row Blues. *This is a continuous line incorporating loops, hearts and stars, and you are free to copy it if you wish.*

Duck and Ducklings

When Jan Allen chose the Duck and Ducklings block for this 36" x 36" quilt she saw it could be made using the squared-up triangles in SaR. We loved the star that emerged, and it looked even better when she added one of her favourite borders – migrating geese! The original bright-coloured quilt is a playmat for a new baby. Jan made a second quilt with pretty floral fabrics to give a soft, floaty, summery, Edwardian feel.

Fabric

Green, yellow, pink and purple: ¼ yard each

Mid blue – ½ yard

Background fabric –1½ yards

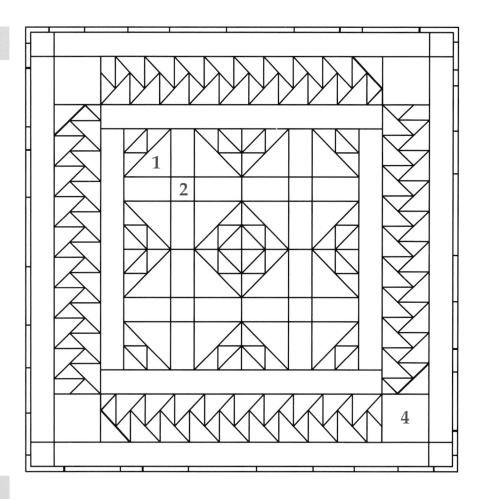

Instructions

Rows are arranged horizontally

1 Half Square Triangles – SaR page 31

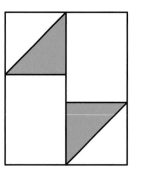

Used as the small squares in the squared-up triangle blocks.
Cut six 2⅞″ squares in pink and six 2⅞″ squares in background to make twelve half square triangles.
Cut two 2⅞″ squares in purple and two 2⅞″ squares in background to make four half square triangles.

Squared-up Triangles – SaR page 37 (using What If...?)

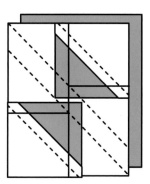

Make twelve in blue/pink.
Make four in green/purple.
Cut 16 rectangles, each 2½″ x 3½″, in background fabric.
Stitch to pink or purple edge of half square triangle.
Cut six 4½″ x 5½″ rectangles in blue.
Cut two 4½″ x 5½″ rectangles in green.
Continue following the instructions in SaR from step 4 (page 36).

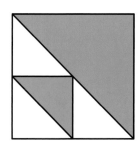

22

Summer Florals, a variation made by Jan Allen.

2 Sashing

Background fabric – cut four 2½″ x 8½″ strips and eight 2½″ x 4½″ rectangles.
Yellow squares – cut four 2½″ squares.
Stitch one square to each end of two 2½″ x 8½″ strips.
Stitch 2½″ x 4½″ rectangles to each end of strips.

3 Assembly

Top and bottom rows are identical 4″ rows. Angle triangle units correctly, following the quilt plan.
Stitch row in following order: triangle unit/ rectangle/two triangles/rectangle/triangle.

Centre 8″ row

Angle triangle units correctly following quilt plan.
Stitch together four green triangles to make centre.
Stitch together two pairs of blue triangles.
Stitch row in following order: pair blue triangles/ 2½″ x 8½″ strip/ centre four triangles/ 2½″ x 8½″ strip/ pair blue triangles.
Adding sashing in between, stitch rows together to make complete centre.

4 Borders

First border

Add 2½″ background fabric border strips all round centre star.

Second border
(Migrating Geese, S&R page 42)

Make 76 x 4″ migrating geese using colours from the star centre; cut 38 squares in background fabric and 19 geese squares. To make one row, stitch 19 completed geese together. Stitch four rows. Stitch one row to opposite sides of quilt.
Cut four 4½″ squares background and add to each end of remaining two migrating geese rows. Stitch these rows to top and bottom of quilt.

Third border

Add 2½″ background fabric border strips with 2½″ square cornerstones in yellow.

Layer, quilt. Bind with remaining colour fabric pieces.

Divers' Delight

There is something about fish that has always held a fascination for me. I love the colours of tropical fish, but my Scandinavian heritage has its own part to play. I find that I often use fish fabrics in my quilts, and enjoy making quilts that have the sea as their theme. *Diver's Delight* uses four Sew-a-Row Quilts techniques to create a delightful wall hanging that can be made in a few hours! When I have taught this as a class I have often found that half the students are divers. An alternative is to use birds as a feature and turn the rows to a vertical setting. The penguin quilt is a super example: the technique is identical, but the quilt is turned at right angles. Did you notice that all three quilts on these pages were made from the same original design?

Fabric

Dark background – ¾ yard

Fish – ½ yard

Border – ½ yard

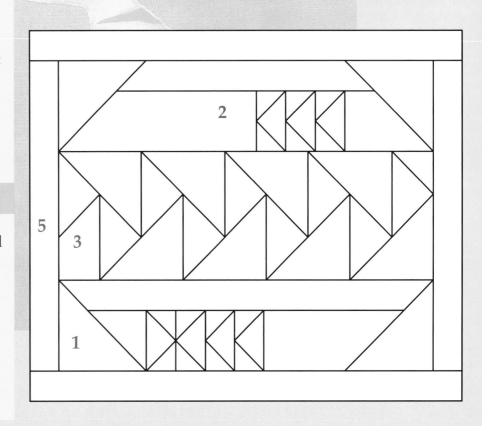

24

Instructions

Rows are arranged horizontally.

1 3D Geese – SaR page 39

Make four 3D geese.
Stitch three geese together; add the fourth goose pointing towards the three.
To complete the bottom row, sew one 7" x 4½" and one 11" x 4½" background strip to either side of geese (smaller piece on left side)

2 Flying Geese – SaR page 40

Use 4" block measurements to make four flying geese.
Choose the best three and stitch together to make top row.
To complete the top row, sew one 7" x 4½" and one 14" x 4½" background strip to either side of geese (smaller piece on right side).

3 Migrating Geese – SaR page 42

Use 8" block measurements.
Use five background squares and three goose squares to make migrating geese.
Choose the best nine and stitch together to make the centre row.

4 Assembly

Stitch flying geese section to top of migrating geese row.
Trim ends in line.
Stitch a 2½" background strip below the migrating geese row. Trim.
Stitch 3D geese row to bottom of quilt. Trim.
Stitch a 2½" background strip above the flying geese row. Trim ends in line.
Press well and square corners.

Above: Julia Reed added more embellishment with appliquéd and embroidered seaweed. Free cut triangles were appliquéd to give the illusion of more fish.

Next page: Another variation, Never Goose A Penguin *by Marion Barnes.*

5 Corners and Borders

Cut four 6" squares from border fabric.
On reverse side of squares mark a diagonal line, corner to corner.
Place one square right sides together in each corner of pieced top. Stitch on lines.
Trim excess fabric leaving a ¼" seam. Press seams out. Square corners.
Cut three 2½" border strips. Stitch border strips to quilt sides. Press seams out. Add top and bottom borders. Press.

6 Appliqué – SaR page 57

Cut out fish and fuse to quilt using the no-sew technique.
Layer, and let your imagination swim in the tropical seas, quilting and embellishing!
Small buttons were used as air bubbles.

An 80" x 88" fantasy quilt that has been lurking in my imagination since I started writing my first book **Sew a Row Quilts**. I was inspired when I saw the Aurora fabric, which to my mind was ideal for the flowing rivers. This set off the whole colour scheme – blues, pinks and mauves, some of my favourites. Mountains and flowers are also present in my hidden valleys, but in exotic hues and shapes. A quilt of peace and tranquillity, with flashes of the unexpected. Read into it what you like, all you budding psychiatrists!

Fabric

Background and binding – 5½ yards

Theme fabric – 2 yards graduated (width of bolt) for river and final border

Assorted colours to match graduated fabric – quarter yards or minimum 5″ squares (for mountains, vine, leaves and flowers)

Freezer paper – 2½ yards

Instructions

Rows are arranged vertically.

1 Rivers – Creative Stencils (QaR page 76)

Enlarge design 200% to fit an 8″ block.
Cut freezer paper 8½″ x 80½″.
Mark on matt side of freezer paper the centre line, length and width.
Using a pencil, trace stencil: start at centre (with the diamond) and work to the end of the paper, ending with an oval. Repeat in the opposite direction.
You should have ten design repeats along the length of paper. Once you are happy with your design, go over the pencil lines with a black felt tip marker.

Cut out three 8½″ x 81″ lengths from background fabric.
Iron freezer paper pattern to wrong side of one 8½″ x 81″ length of fabric, leaving a small fabric excess either end.

On *right* side of fabric mark the stencil pattern using a semi-permanent fabric marker. You may need a light box to help you see the original pattern black lines.
Peel off freezer paper.

Repeat with a second length. These two are identical, and will form the rivers at the sides of the quilt.

To make the centre river, cut the original paper pattern through the centre and tape the oval ends together to make a new centre.

Iron to wrong side of third 8½″ x 81″ length of fabric, again leaving a small fabric excess either end. On right side of fabric mark the stencil pattern.

Reverse Appliqué – QaR page 83

Cut six 8½″ strips across the width of the graduated theme fabric.
Remove selvedges. Stitch two widths together

28

end to end to give flowing colour effect. Repeat. These two will become the side rivers. Press seams open.

For centre river, stitch remaining two widths, inverting colours. Press seam open.
Place graduated fabric right side up. Place marked background fabric right side up on top of graduated fabric matching raw edges. Pin/baste in place and reverse appliqué by hand or machine.
Optional – remove excess theme fabric to avoid quilting problems associated with two fabric layers.
Trim ends to measure 80½" length.

2 Delectable Mountains – SaR page 32

Make 60 x 4" blocks using dark background and lights in colours that match theme fabric. Stitch ten together to make a row. Sew six rows.

3 Vine and flowers

Cut two 12½" x 80½" lengths background fabric.

Easy Stems – SaR page 62

Prepare two vines approximately 80" long. Appliqué each to the two background lengths.

English Patchwork – SaR page 65

Make ten flowers using the 1" mitre template, and referring to page 69 if you wish to add new angles to this patchwork.

Appliqué one to each end of vines, and place remaining six randomly along each vine. Each vine has five flowers.

Leaves – SaR page 64

Cut out 20 leaves and appliqué ten to each vine.

Row assembly

Stitch delectable mountains rows to either side of river rows, taking care with alignment. Stitch all rows together, again taking care of alignment.

Close-up showing a fantasy flower.

4 Borders

First border

Stitch 4½" background border strips on all sides of quilt.

Layer and quilt. Quilting in the ditch has been done around each mountain. A meander quilting design has been used in the river and vine rows.

Second border

Square quilt, and add a final pleated border using a 1¼" graduated fabric strip folded right sides out and pressed. Stay stitch to edges of quilt.

Add binding (SaR page 98).

Mountains and Rivers, *a variation on* Enchanted Valleys, *also by Karin Hellaby.*

QH tips

To help with seam alignment - use a chalk marker to place a mark in seam allowance of stencil row directly opposite diamond tip. This should then be aligned with the side of a mountain. Use a walking foot to stitch rows together to prevent slippage.

Machine stitch along the marked stencil pattern. Then you can trim the top fabric close to this line of stitching and cover the raw edge with satin stitch (see below).

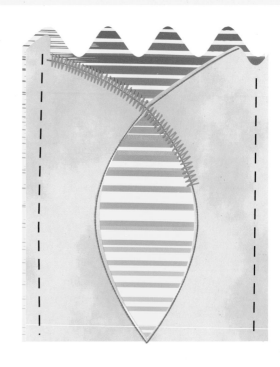

This close-up shows the use of satin stitch for reverse appliqué on the river row.

What if...

...you used a machine embroidery edge stitch instead of satin stitch – buttonhole, for instance?

...you reverse stitched by hand?

...you emphasised the finished river edges with couched embroidery threads?

...you quilted ripples down the centre of the rivers?

...you used another stencil as a flowing river?

...you used bias binding tape for the banks of the river?

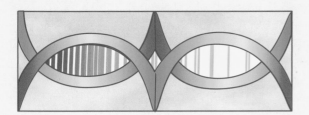

I Spy a Rainbow

Spring morning in the garden, full of fresh colours as the flowers emerge after winter. The original quilt by Ann Harper (see p. 33) was her first, and inspired this fun learning quilt for children: and what better way than a new slant on 'I Spy'? This quilt can start many other games: how about 'snap' (finding matching animals in the patchwork); naming and remembering the rainbow colours; or matching colours between borders and geese? As you can see, this simple 41" x 51" quilt by Anne Smith can look very different depending on the fabrics you choose.

31

Fabric

Rainbow colours: ¼ yard each of red, orange, yellow, green, blue, indigo, and violet

Dresdens (eighth fabric): ⅛ yard or scraps of extra red needed for eighth spoke

Theme fabric: 1 yard, including border and binding

Background fabric: 1 yard

Centre row background – ¼ yard

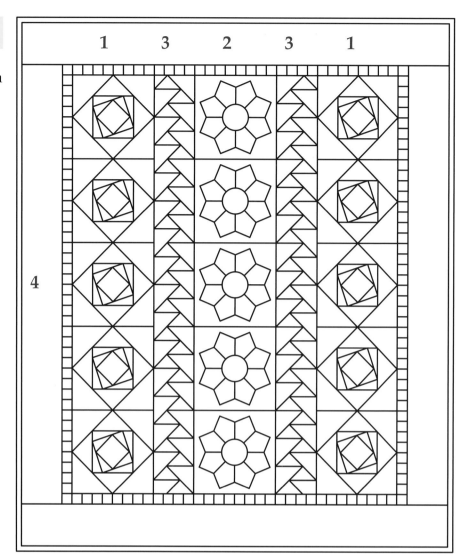

Instructions

Rows are arranged vertically.

1 **Dancing Squares Foundation Fun – SaR page 52**
Enlarge foundation pattern 200% to fit an 8" block.
Stitch ten Dancing Squares blocks, using theme fabric in centre squares and surrounding this with rainbow colours.
Stitch five blocks together for each row.

2 **Dresden Daisy – SaR page 70**

Make five Dresden Daisies. Use eight colours for the petals. Appliqué a circle of theme fabric in the centre of each daisy.
Stitch each completed daisy to an 8½" background square.
Stitch blocks together to make centre row.

32

3 Migrating Geese – *SaR* page 42

Use 4″ block cutting measurement for migrating geese.
Cut 30 background squares and 15 rainbow-coloured geese squares.
Use to make 60 migrating geese.
Stitch 30 together to make each row.
Stitch vertical rows together following quilt plan.

4 Borders

First border

Quick strip pieced border (*SaR* page 85).
Cut a 1½″ strip from all seven rainbow colours.
Stitch together as a strip set. Press.
Cut 1½″ sections at right angles to strip set and join end to end to make borders.

Second border

Add a 4½″ theme fabric border.

Layer, quilt and add binding.

Top right: Close-up of a Dresden Daisy from I Spy a Rainbow.

Bottom right: Spring Morning *by Ann Harper, the inspiration for* I Spy a Rainbow.

Chinese Rows

Val Derks is a regular tutor at Quilters Haven and won a Quilt Expo 2002 award, so I challenged her to design a row quilt. Her inspiration for this quilt was 'seeing' delectable mountains as Chinese lanterns. Blue and white batiks were selected for an oriental feel. We loved the shape of the flowers, made from five heart petals.

In the centre of the floral row is patchwork that is open to different interpretations. Are they 'vases'? Or a path with flower beds on each side?

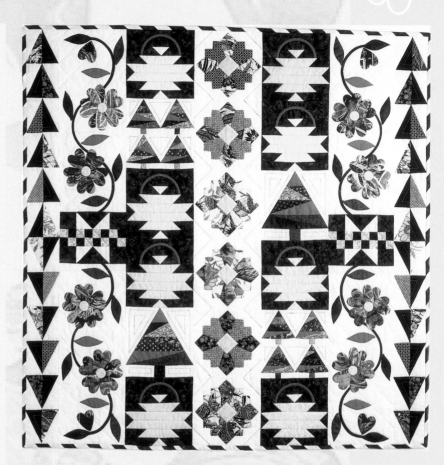

Fabric

Light background – 2 yards

Main blue – ½ yard

Various blues – 7 x ¼ yards

Various yellows – 4 x ¼ yards

Various greens – ¼ yards and scraps

1 2 3 4 3 2 1

Instructions

Rows are arranged vertically.

1 Skinny Triangles – SaR page 35

Make 24 blocks using the **What If...**, sewing 24 left and 24 right units to make 24 isosceles triangle blocks. Stitch 12 blocks to make one row, following quilt plan. Make two rows.

2 Chequerboard – SaR page 20

Cut two 1½" strips, one in dark and one in light. Cut 16 x 1½" sections. Stitch eight into a chequerboard row. Make two rows.

Geese – SaR page 40
Make four dark geese from a 4" block.
Cut eight 2½" dark squares. Stitch to either side of single goose.
Stitch a chequerboard between two geese/square units. Repeat.

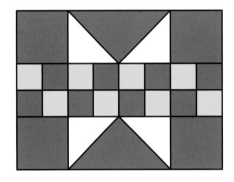

Easy Stems – SaR page 62
Make four 28" length stems.
Cut four 21½" x 8½" background rectangles.
Appliqué one stem to each rectangle.

Appliqué – SaR page 56
Cut 44 hearts. Appliqué five hearts to make one flower, add a yellow centre.

QH tip

Use a pudding bowl to draw a stem placement guide on the background, turning the bowl as you draw around the rim.

Follow quilt plan to position appliqués.
Appliqué eight flowers to background, two flowers along each stem. Cut 28 leaves.
Appliqué seven leaves on each background.
Appliqué remaining hearts.

3 Delectable Mountains – SaR page 32

Make 32 x 4" blocks in yellow and dark fabric (do not add side background strip).
Stitch four blocks together to make a Chinese lantern.
Cut eight 2½" x 8½" dark rectangles; stitch one to the top of each lantern.
Appliqué one 8" easy stem handle to each lantern.

Foundation Fun – SaR page 48
Make two 8" and eight 4" trees – SaR page 52.
Stitch 4" trees into two blocks.
Stitch blocks into row following quilt plan.

4 Dresden Diamond – SaR page 72

Make six Dresden Diamond blocks. Stitch together to make centre row.
Stitch rows together following quilt plan.
Layer, quilt.
A glittery thread was machine quilted around each patchwork shape and used to repeat shapes in light areas. Cross hatch background quilting was used in flower row.
Bind using double fold binding cut from a two colour 2" strips set. Binding strips are cut at a 45° angle to give the lovely bias effect.

Christmas Quilt

Christmas provides a wonderful excuse to change the home decor and hang a whole new set of quilts. We had to include a festive project because we love to use all those yummy Christmas fabrics. If you love embellishment then this 47" x 51" quilt is a great project for adding all those fun buttons and glittery ribbons and thread. Both projects were made by Julia Reed, to designs by Karin Hellaby.

Fabric

Christmas fabrics – various in ½ and ¼ yards

Background whites and creams in various shades – 2 yards

Green border and binding – ¾ yard

Instructions

1 Star row

Cut three 4½" squares in star fabric. Cut twelve 2½" squares in background fabric. Make twelve 4" flying geese (SaR page 40), cutting three 5¼" geese squares in Christmas background fabric and twelve 2⅞" squares in star fabrics.

Stitch background square to each side of six finished geese.

1

2

3

4

5

6

36

Stitch one goose to each side of star square. To top and bottom add a goose/ squares unit.
Cut two 4½″ x 8½″ background rectangles. Assemble row by stitching stars alternating with 4½″ x 8½″ background rectangles.
Appliqué a star onto centre star square (CaR page 64).

2 Christmas trees

Tree – CaR page 52.
Make eight using 4″ foundation template but cutting main section of tree as a whole.
Embellish to look like Christmas trees.
Stitch together to make row.

3 Holly row

Cut 16 x 4½″ squares in assorted backgrounds.
Stitch four squares together to make a block. Make four blocks.

Suffolk Puffs (CaR page 63)

Make twelve using a 2″ template.
Cut out 16 holly leaves.
Appliqué four holly leaves and three Suffolk Puffs (CaR page 63) onto each block.
Stitch blocks together to make row.

4 Gingerbread Men

Cut out eight gingerbread men. Cut out eight 4½″ background squares.
Appliqué one gingerbread man onto each of seven squares. Use a pigma pen to mark eyes and mouth.
Stitch eight squares together to make a row. The eighth gingerbread man is placed in a stocking!

QH tip

Stitch larger strips than needed to top and sides of parcels. Then trim to 8½″ square.

5 Stockings

Cut out eight stockings using template.
Cut out eight 4½″ background squares.
Appliqué one stocking onto each square.
Add a gingerbread man to one stocking.
Stitch together to make row.

6 Parcels

Piece a square and/ or a rectangle parcel into an 8½″ square. Parcels are cut: 5½″ x 6½″; 3¼″ x 5¼″; 4½″ x 4½″; 4½″ x 6½″; and 5½″ x 5½″.
Add background strips to make an 8½″ square.
Embellish with ribbon to look like parcels.
Stitch rows together to make quilt top.

7 Borders

First border: Chop Suey (CaR page 22).
Make 38 x 4½″ blocks.
Create two rows of nine blocks and two rows of ten.
Attach the shorter rows to the sides of the quilt, and the longer rows to top and bottom.

Second border: Flying geese (CaR page 40).
Make 42 x 4″ geese. Stitch two rows of eleven geese and stitch to each side of quilt.
Stitch two rows of ten geese.

Half square triangles (CaR page 31):
Make four using 2⅞″ squares. Stitch one to each end of the two ten geese rows.
Stitch to top and bottom of quilt top.

Third border: Add 2½″ strips.

Layer and quilt. Bind in fabric that matches border geese.

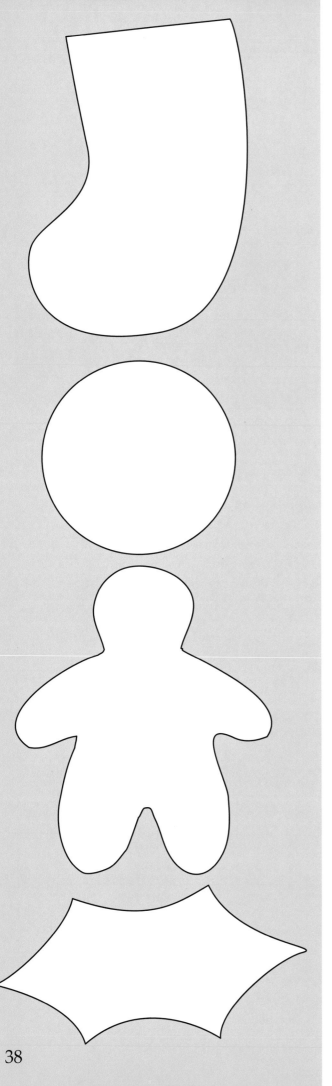

Christmas Table Runner

Make five 4″ blocks. Stitch together.
Add a 4″ chop suey border to both sides.
Cut a 9″ background square, and cut
diagonally to make two triangles. Stitch to
each end of runner.
Add a star, and appliqué.

What if...

A small gift were inserted into each
stocking?

Sam's Chickens

It is thrilling to be told you have inspired someone! Jenny Cooper, a young mother, attended a lecture I gave about SaR. Afterwards she turned to the lady next to her and said she never thought she would be able to make a quilt, but she would have a go! She started with a few quarters of chicken fabric that she knew her son Sam, aged four, liked. "I wanted to try as many different rows as possible and tried to use fabric best suited to each technique. This is very much a 'make it up as you go along' quilt. I called it *Sam's Chickens* because I have no imagination for witty titles." I hope Jenny's 60" x 90" quilt inspires many others to try quiltmaking.

Fabric

Quarter and half yards in
various fabrics.

Instructions

Rows are arranged horizontally

1 **Flying Geese – SaR page 40**

Make 24 geese using 4″ block
measurement. Sew into row.

2 **Greek Keys – SaR page 28**

Make 24 Greek keys using 4″ block
measurement. Refer to diagram on SaR
page 29 for placement.
Stitch twelve together to make one row.
Repeat to make two rows. Stitch rows
together.

3 **Trees – Foundation Fun – SaR page 52**

Make 12 trees using 4″ block. Sew into row.

4 **Appliqué – SaR page 56**

Cut or piece together background 48½″ x 8½″.
Cut out ten birds using template and appliqué
to background using quilt plan as a guide.

5 **Dancing Squares – SaR page 52**

Twelve dancing squares are made using 4″
block where the centre square is larger.
Place a 2½″ feature square in centre to cover
pieces 1–9. Sew squares into row.

6 **Alternating Four Patch.
Chequerboard – SaR page 20**

Use two 2½″ contrasting strips to make twelve
four patch blocks.
Cut twelve 4½″ squares in feature fabric.
Alternate with four patch to stitch into
an 8″ row.

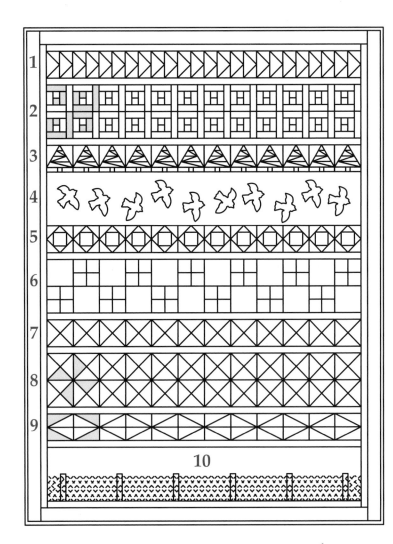

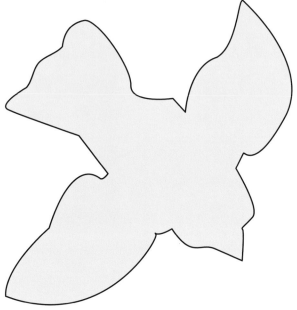

QH tip

While creating the wire netting use a
stabiliser such as thin paper or 'Stitch
and tear' to prevent stitches from rippling
fabric.

7 Quarter Square Triangles – SaR page 34

Make twelve quarter square triangles using 4″ block measurement. Sew into row.

8 Pinwheels – Quarter Square Triangles (SaR page 34 using What If...?)

Make 24 quarter square triangles, each square has three background triangles and one dark.

9 Skinny Triangles – SaR page 35 using What If...?

Make 24 skinny triangles. Stitch together into row of isosceles triangles with lights forming centre diamond. Appliqué one Suffolk puff and three leaves into each centre diamond formed from triangles.

10 Chicken pen

Cut or piece together background 48½″ x 8½″ using a chicken feature fabric.
Cut out six fence post rectangles 4″ x ¾″. Appliqué fence posts, following quilt plan. Create the wire netting using a three stage stretch stitch as a ¾″ diagonal cross hatch design.

11 Assembly

Cut 1½″ strips fabric for sashing.
Following quilt plan, stitch rows together with sashing in between to make quilt top.

12 Borders

First border: add 1½″ sashing fabric border strips.

Second border: add 2½″ border strips.

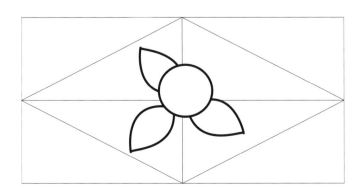

Reversible Quilt-as-you-go

Every now and then I have one of those 'Eureka' moments and this 49" x 59" quilt is the result of one of them. One of my students was struggling with a reversible quilt project and I said it would be easier using a SaR technique. No sooner were the words out of my mouth than I was challenged to make one. Here is my version using the Sew and Flip quilt layering technique, and taking it a step further. I chose to use homespun flannels, which have a stretchy quality that can make construction a challenge! Even so, they give this lap quilt a wonderful cuddly feel. Of course if you don't fancy trying a reversible quilt-as-you-go then this project will give you two quilts which can be finished traditionally.

Fabric (dark side)

Light homespun flannels – 8 light quarter yards

Dark homespun flannels – 12 dark quarter yards, includes binding

1 Roman Stripes (SaR page 24)

Make 44 x 4″ block Roman Stripes using a four strip set in darks. A light 3½″ strip is used as the triangle background in the block.
Carefully, stitch squares together into a row of eleven blocks, following quilt plan.
Stitch four rows.
Stay stitch ⅛″ from raw edge of each row to prevent stretching of bias edges.

2 Squares

Cut 28 x 4½″ dark squares and 27 x 4½″ light squares.
Appliqué a light heart to ten dark squares (SaR page 64).
Stitch squares together into a row of eleven blocks, alternating light/dark as in quilt plan.
Distribute appliqué squares randomly within rows keeping to light/dark placement.

If you are following quilt-as-you-go, do *not* stitch rows and borders together at this stage.

3 Borders

First border: cut 2½″ strips in various light fabrics. Make up four lengths, one for each quilt side.

Second border: Piano keys – (SaR page 85)
Cut 2½″ strips in various dark fabrics. Stitch together to make a strip set. Cut 4½″ sections and sew into border strips.
Make up four border strips: side borders have 22 piano keys. Top and bottom borders each have 24 piano keys.
Stitch a border 1 to each piano keys side border. Stitch one piano key to each end of remaining two borders, and stitch to top and bottom piano keys borders.

Fabric (light side)

Minimum width 45"

¾ yard each in two lights

¾ yard each in two darks includes binding

½ yard centre dark and first border

Instructions (light side)

1 Cut...

...five 4½" x 44½" lengths in darks and four 4½" x 44½" lengths in lights.

2 Appliqué (SaR page 56)

Cut out nine stars in lights and nine stars in darks. Buttonhole appliqué stars to cut lengths. If you are following quilt-as-you-go, do *not* stitch rows and borders together at this stage.

3 Borders

First border: cut 2½" strips in a dark fabric.

Second border: Chequerboard (SaR page 20)

Cut 2½" strips from dark and light fabrics. Stitch into chequerboard patchwork border strips. Side borders have 22 pairs. Top and bottom borders have 24 pairs Stitch a dark first border strip to each chequerboard border. Assembly using quilt-as-you-go is a method of attaching rows on both sides of the quilt at the same time. As the rows are attached by stitching through the wadding (60" x 70" medium weight cotton wadding which can be ironed) the quilt will be 'quilted'. It is essential to use a walking foot if you are machine sewing seams by this method.

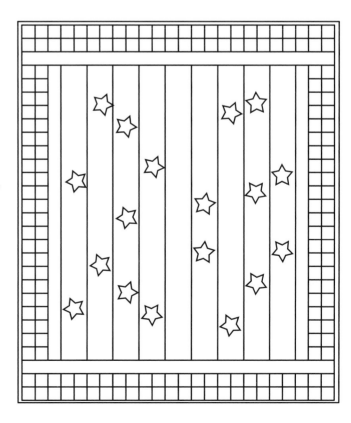

44

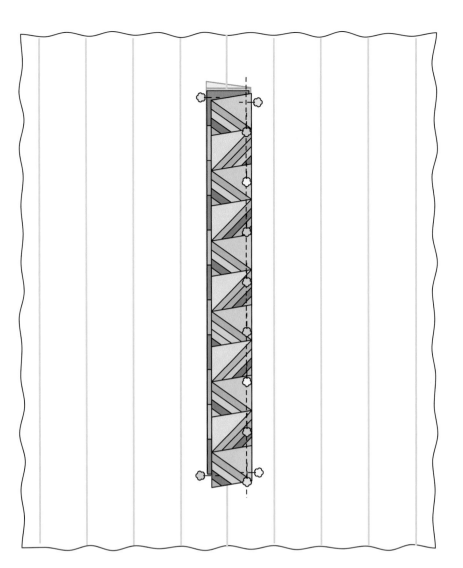

Diagram to help you see how rows on both sides of the wadding are attached in the 'quilt as you go' technique.

Assembly

1 **Layering with flip and sew (SaR page 88)**

Mark one side of wadding with a centre vertical line, plus four more vertical lines in each direction 6" apart.

Place the centre two dark side rows right sides together on marked side of wadding, aligning with centre vertical line. Pin to wadding at right angles to fabric edge. Then use long flower pins to mark long raw edge of fabric through wadding so that pins can be seen on reverse side. Pin corner raw edges using pins placed at right angles.

Carefully turn over. Use the pin markers to place two centre light rows right side together so that they are exactly on reverse of dark rows. Pin, baste and then stitch seams, sewing four layers of fabric and wadding all at the same time. Press both sides well, pressing rows away from centre.

QH tip

Use cotton wadding and a machine walking foot for reversible assembly.

Continue to stitch additional rows in each direction from centre always sewing one seam to attach rows both sides and wadding. I use the following techniques.
On light side press attached row away, then pin and stay stitch close to raw edge. Pin next light row right sides down on top of stay stitched row, aligning raw edges. Turn to dark side pin next pair dark rows to wadding using stay stitch line for alignment. Baste if this helps to keep the rows aligned. Stitch in place. Press rows away from centre.
Continue until all rows are in place.
Attach the border using the same techniques, side borders first, then top and bottom borders.

2 **Reversible Binding (SaR page 95)**

Quilter's Tote Bag

Store your rotary cutting equipment in this handy tote. You will be the envy of all the other students attending classes when you walk in with one of these easily assembled bags. Ideal for using the short rows that you want to try. This project started off as a small quilt, fold in half and stitch up the sides and you have the general idea. We added an inner pocket to hold your ruler. This size tote holds a 22" x 18" mat and 6" x 24" ruler. The cutter is best stored in your sewing box.

Tote bag by Pat Matthes

Fabric

Lining, pocket – 1½ yards

Borders, binding and handles – ¾ yard

Fabric for 24 x 4" blocks and six 8" blocks

Cotton wadding 36" x 45"

Cutting

Lining: 31" x 41"

Pocket: 16" x 30"

Borders and sashing: five 2½" strips

Binding: four 2¼" strips from fabric width

Handles: two 4½" strips approximately 2" long

Wadding: one 31" x 41" and two 1¼" x 27" strips for handles

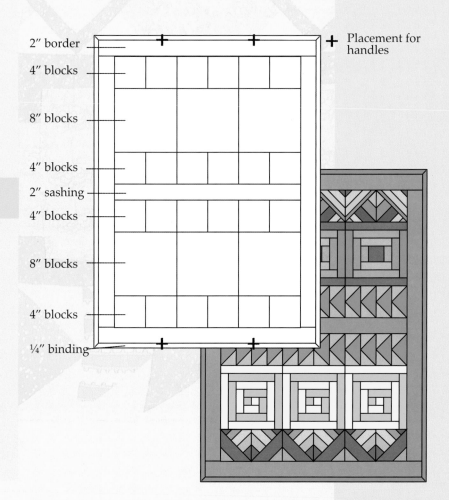

2" border

4" blocks

8" blocks

4" blocks

2" sashing

4" blocks

8" blocks

4" blocks

¼" binding

Placement for handles

46

Instructions

1 Using any techniques in Sew a Row Quilts...

...make six 8″ blocks and 24 x 4″ blocks.
Stitch two horizontal rows of three 8″ blocks and four rows of six 4″ blocks.

2 Stitch rows together...

...as in the quilt-plan diagram with a 2″ sashing strip in the middle.

3 Add a 2″ border to each side...

...and a 2″ border to the top and bottom.

4 Layer the quilt...

...as directed on SaR page 86.

5 Secure the layers and quilt...

...as desired before stitching the layers together on the outside edge. Trim away the surplus lining and wadding.

6 Pocket

Fold in half along the length, right sides out, press well. Topstitch the folded edge and neaten the two long raw edges together. Place the pocket on the lining side, as shown in the diagram, pin, turn over and stitch in the ditch, from patchwork side. Remove the pins; fold the pocket up. Pin and stitch to the sides and trim away the surplus fabric.

7 Bind the edges...

...following the instructions on SaR page 98.

8 Fold the quilt in half right side out

Stitch the sides together from the top edge to the fold at the bottom. Stitch just inside the binding, a zipper machine foot helps you stitch close to the binding. You may wish to start 2″ from the top. Reinforce at the top if desired.

9 Handles

Place the wadding ¼″ away from the one long edge, fold the fabric over the wadding and turn under the surplus. Turn in the raw edges at each end and topstitch the folded under edge, repeat on the opposite side. Stitch them as indicated on the diagram, approximately 6″ from tote sides.

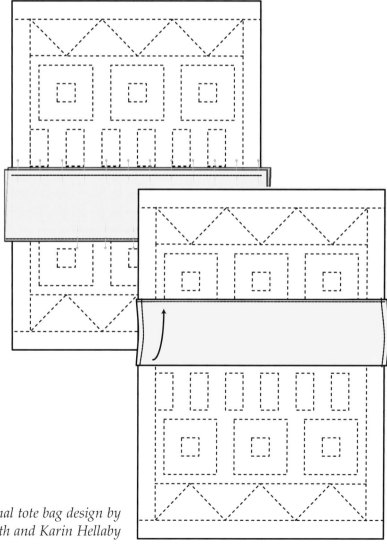

Original tote bag design by Anne Smith and Karin Hellaby

*Tote bag by Ann Whatling
showing front and reverse sides*

*Above: reverse of tote
bag by Pat Matthes*

*Right: Tote bag by
Liz Powell*

What if...

...you sewed a velcro or toggle fastening to close the top of
the tote bag? Added more pockets for various rulers?

48

Funky Folders

Marion Barnes, one of the staff at Quilters Haven, suggested fabric covered folders as a 'Make and Take' session at one of our shop Open Days. They proved to be so popular that we were asked for instructions. I thought it would be fun to include patchwork blocks to give that extra personal touch. We have included many ideas to create folders for specific purposes and in different sizes. If you want a gift idea for 'someone who has everything' then this is ideal. It is also a great idea for getting kids interested in crafts.

Materials

To make a folder with a finished size of 8½" x 12" (A4)

Firm cardboard 12" x 17½" (we recommend grey board or art display board)

Cover and inner lining – ½ yard fabric

Instant tacky fabric glue

½ yard fusible paper (such as Steam-a-Seam 2)

12" x 17½" thin wadding

Top folder by Pat Matthes

Bottom folder by Carole Redman

Instructions

1 Card preparation

Mark cardboard centre along short width (spine).
Draw a line ½ inch either side of centre, and then a second line ¼ inch outside of these two lines (see diagram).
Score down these four lines (ignoring centre line) with a small rotary cutter, craft knife, or *hera* marker, but don't cut right through.
Fold along the scored lines until a book 'shape' is made.
A piece of thin wadding is glued to the outside before the cover fabric is attached, this gives a nice, soft feel to the finished book cover.

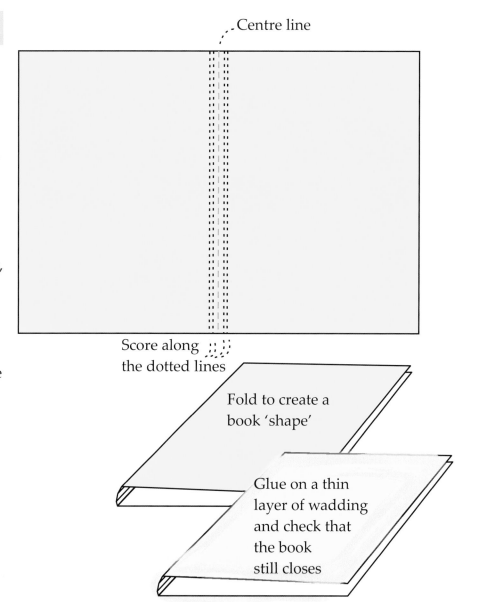

Centre line

Score along the dotted lines

Fold to create a book 'shape'

Glue on a thin layer of wadding and check that the book still closes

2 Patchwork cover

The outside cover measures 13½" x 19½" before completion, 12" x 17½" on completion.
Make three 4" patchwork blocks and stitch into row.
Add a 1" strip to short ends of row (this becomes the turn under on the inside).
Stitch a 2" x 13½" fabric strip along length of patchwork row on right hand side.
Stitch a 14" x 13½" fabric strip along length of patchwork row on left hand side. Trim all ends even.
Cut 11½" x 17" inner lining fabric. Bond the lining fabric to one side of the fusible paper.

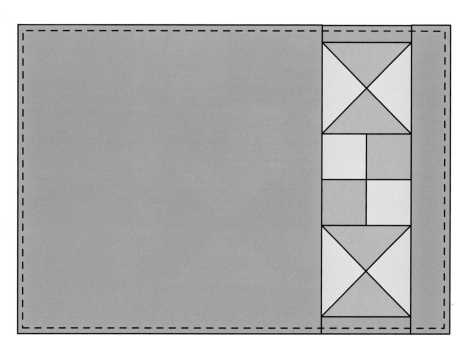

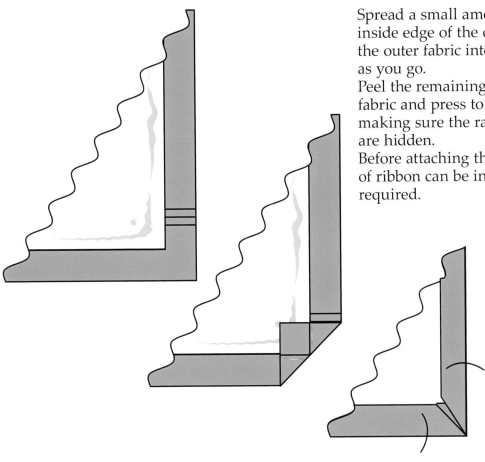

Spread a small amount of glue around the inside edge of the cardboard shape and stick the outer fabric into place, mitreing the corners as you go.

Peel the remaining paper from bonded lining fabric and press to the inside of the cover making sure the raw edges of the outer cover are hidden.

Before attaching the lining a small piece of ribbon can be inserted to make a tie if required.

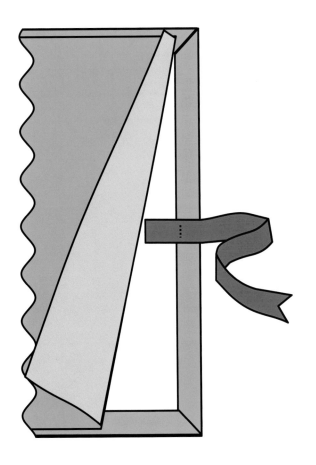

3 Ideas for closures and uses

Insert 2 lengths of ribbon/string/cord in between lining and outer front and back covers to make a simple tie.

A button can be sewn to the top outer cover to wind ribbon around to fasten.

If the lining is made from fabric covered card it is easy to make eyelets to thread ribbon through to attach loose-leaf paper.

'Two way' glue can be purchased from art shops and can be used to temporarily attach paperback books or note pads to the inside of the back cover. It is fun to make a themed cover to match the book, Yorkshire Moor print fabric for instance, for a copy of *Wuthering Heights*!

Ring binder mounts can be bought from stationery suppliers and stitched/glued inside. Tie a length of elasticised cord around the spine and use it to keep a notebook in place.

What If...

You wanted to make folders in other sizes?

Decide on the finished size of the cover. Double this and add one inch to width measurement. Cut cardboard to this size. Fabric for cover is cut one inch larger than card size, all round. Inner lining fabric is cut ¼″ smaller than card size all round.

Folders by Carole Redman (back, left and right) and Janet Last (front)

Home Sweet Home

Don't you just love it when you design a quilt and someone else takes your instructions and makes a better quilt? Not only one but two great quilts! Julia Reed's two 25" x 29" quilts depict the theme in night and day. As her favourite is the birdhouses against a night sky, I have used this for the instructions. Birdhouses are a popular patchwork project and yours can be personalised to reflect your home and garden.

Fabric

½ yard background fabric (sky)

½ yard second border and binding

½ yard grass, stems and leaves

Quarter yards for birdhouses, bird house poles, birds, stars and moon

Instructions

1 Houses

Cut three 4½" squares.

2 Roofs

3D geese ℒaℛ page 39. Make three geese and sew one on top of each house square.

3 Bird House Poles

Cut two 2" x 22" sky and one 1½" x 22" pole. Sew together along length with pole fabric between sky fabrics. Press.
Cut into three lengths – 10½", 6" and 4". Sew each cut length to the base of a bird house.

4 Doors

Suffolk Puffs (ℒaℛ page 63). Cut three 4" diameter circles. Stitch onto centre of bird house squares.

5 Flock of Birds

Half square triangles (ℒaℛ page 31), to use in squared up triangles.
Make three squares by cutting two 2⅞" squares sky and two 2⅞" squares blue. This will produce four 2½" half square triangles. Pick the best three.

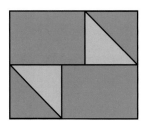
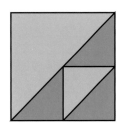

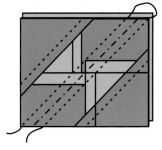

The original Home Sweet Home
by Karin Hellaby.

Squared up triangles (ℒaR page 36)

Cut four 2½″ x 3½″ rectangles. Stitch one to one side of each half square triangle. Follow instructions from ℒaR steps 3–7. Cut two 5½″ x 4½″ rectangles blue to proceed with step 8. Choose three squared up triangle units to use and discard fourth.

6 Vertical rows completion

Work rows starting from left.
Row 1: cut one 2½″ x 21½″ strip sky (background).
Row 2: cut one 4½″ x 10″ sky. Stitch to top of medium length birdhouse.
Row 3: cut one 4½″ x 5″ sky. Stitch to top of longest length birdhouse.
Row 4: cut one 2½″ x 21½″ strip sky.
Row 5: cut one 4½″ x 8″ sky. Add one squared up triangle unit.
Row 6: cut one 4½″ x 13½″ sky. Add two squared up triangle units.
Stitch completed rows together to make quilt top.
Trim rows even.

7 Vine

Easy Stem ℒaR page 62.

Cut one 1″ x 12″ bias strip. Stitch in place from base of tallest bird house pole along length of pole.
ℒaR page 64 use templates to cut a variety of leaves. Cut out three birds.
Use your favourite appliqué method to stitch leaves, cat, moon and stars in place.

Grass border

Cut one 4½″ x 20″ strip fabric. Stitch to base of quilt top. Square quilt corners before adding the borders.

8 Borders

Border 1: Cut 1″ strips and add to quilt.

Border 2: Cut 2½″ strips and add to quilt.

Layer and quilt. This quilt was machine quilted using a random meandering pattern. Stem stitch embroidery was added as tendrils on the stems.

Embellish!

Home Sweet Home – Daytime *by Julia Reed*

Template

Use a plate or saucer to draw out sun or moon templates. And as for the embellishments on the quilt on this page...!

Embellishments

Fun embellishments are a feature of this book – and the right fabric can also make an enormous difference to these projects. So what is the right fabric? Simply the one that is right for you – that speaks to your sense of colour and design, or has a particular meaning for you and your family.

Here we feature some of the fabrics and embellishments from the projects made for this book, just to give you a few ideas and, we hope, lots of inspiration!

Can you see which projects they come from...?

About the designs

I can only doodle rough design sketches, as I am certainly no artist in the traditional sense! Put it this way – my students have never felt intimidated by my drawings. Often my ideas are inspired by a new fabric I have just got to use.

From the original sketch, I start to cut and sew blocks. I don't sew them together into rows until I have asked family, staff, students and even customers for their thoughts. Often I receive many ideas that help to develop the project further. I don't often work in isolation, and to me, patchwork and quilting is about enjoying the company of a group of like-minded people who are all helping each other.

About the author

Karin Hellaby was born in the north-east of England of Norwegian parents: her first language was Norwegian. She studied for a Home Economics teaching degree from the University of Wales. She now lives in Suffolk, UK, and is the single parent of three wonderful sons.

Karin started teaching quiltmaking around her kitchen table when pregnant with her third son, Alexander, who is now 13 years old. Quilters Haven opened in 1993 as a teaching centre, with a shop alongside to supply the students, a unique concept in England at that time. It moved to its 17th-century timber-framed building in 1996. The attractive shop, with gallery room and teaching area, attracts quiltmakers and teachers from all over the world. In 1998 Karin, with the help of her son Ross (then aged 15), won the Kile Scholarship – International Retailer of the Year. The next step was to write a book. That was **Sew a Row Quilts**!

As a shop owner and teacher, Karin is in a position where she can sometimes see when a new book is needed. **Magic Pillows, Hidden Quilts** was written for such a gap. She loves travelling and has enjoyed teaching at the International quilt markets and festivals in the USA and Europe.

58

Addresses

For all your sewing needs

Quilters Haven
68 High Street, Wickham Market
Suffolk IP13 0QU, UK

Tel: +44 (0)1728 746275
Fax: +44 (0)1728 746314

Shop opening hours: 9 am – 5 pm,
Monday to Saturday
(Some evening and Sunday openings
dependent on class schedules)

Fully secure on-line shop on:
www.quilters-haven.co.uk

E-mail: quilters.haven@btinternet.com

Custom machine quilting

Quilting Solutions
Firethorn, Rattlesden Road,
Drinkstone,
Bury St Edmunds,
Suffolk IP30 9TL

Tel: +44 (0)1449 736280
Web: www.quiltingsolutions.co.uk

(Quilting of *Sew a Row Blues* and
Enchanted Valleys)

Design and layout

Creative Computing
Rosemary Muntus and Allan Scott
Old Mill House, The Causeway,
Hitcham, Suffolk IP7 7NF, UK

Tel: +44 (0)1449 741747

E-mail: design@thecraftycomputer.com
Web: www.thecraftycomputer.co.uk

Distribution outside the UK

Quilters' Resource Inc.
PO Box 148850
Chicago
Illinois 60614
USA

Tel: 773-278-5695
Fax: 773-278-1348

Web: www.quiltersresource.com

More books by Karin Hellaby

To use this book properly you *must* have a copy of **Sew a Row Quilts**: so we hope you've already shared the experience of quilters all over the world who have used Karin's first book to sew patchwork blocks into rows, and then sew the rows together into a quilt top.

The **Sew a Row** magic formula gives you the block sizes and the structure that you need.

Clear diagrams and step-by-step explanations show you how you can achieve simple, quick and well-proven patchwork techniques.

The results are spectacular – yet they're efficient both with fabric and with time.

With **Sew a Row** you really are never too busy to make a quilt!

'The clear illustrations and fifteen plus examples of students' row quilts make this a book which demands to be used immediately. Excellent.'

Eleanor Reynolds, *Popular Patchwork* magazine

Open a pillow to magically reveal a spectacular quilt! Have fun with the three very different magic pillows – and learn how to mix and match patchwork blocks to create your own designs, quickly and easily, using the latest machine sewing techniques.

Just like the other books in this series, **Magic Pillows, Hidden Quilts** provides clear diagrams and step-by-step instructions, with:

- 20 projects for you to try

- 3 different magic pillows: slip-in, wrap-around and quillow

- Fast and easy techniques laid out as lap size and mini quilts

- A dozen different blocks – and thousands of combinations – to make your quilt unique!